ENGLISH ARCHITECTURAL DRAWING

MEDIEVAL CRAFTSMEN AND DESIGN

ENGLISH ARCHITECTURAL DRAWING

MEDIEVAL CRAFTSMEN AND DESIGN

Arnold Pacey

© Arnold Pacey, 2015

Published by Arnold Pacey

A CIP catalogue record for this book is available from the British Library.

ISBN 978-0-9932875-0-3

Book layout and cover design by Clare Brayshaw

Cover photographs
Detail of an inscribed drawing at Gloucester (photo: Paul Barnwell).

Fireplace in the Parliament Room at Gloucester Cathedral with numerous inscribed drawings on its overmantel (photo: Paul Barnwell)

Window at Christchurch Priory, Hampshire, for which there is a related drawing inside the building (photo: Philip Pacey)

Prepared and printed by:

York Publishing Services Ltd
64 Hallfield Road
Layerthorpe
York YO31 7ZQ

Tel: 01904 431213

Website: www.yps-publishing.co.uk

CONTENTS

Preface

This short book can be read as an introductory account of drawings used in England by medieval masons and builders. However, it is also intended as a supplement to an earlier, larger book, *Medieval Architectural Drawing: English Craftsmen's Methods* (hereafter abbreviated to *Medieval Drawing*, or *MD*) and it reviews drawings discovered or reinterpreted since the former work was published in 2007.

The main aim of that book and this supplement is to establish how many medieval architectural drawings survive in England (but not the rest of the British Isles). It reviews them according to various categories such as working drawings or geometrical drawings. Bearing in mind that few architectural drawings on parchment are to be found in archives, the emphasis is on establishing how many exist on tracing floors and in other places used by medieval masons.

The gazetteer at the end of the book lists about forty sites where drawings have been found. There is more than one drawing in some places, notably York Minster, where five identifiable drawings can be seen on the tracing floor, together with unidentified fragments of many others. In addition, the gazetteer lists one or two drawings that are significant for other reasons but are not strictly drawings related to architectural design or construction. Thus the number of *architectural* drawings represented in the gazetteer is around 45, of which more than half, about 24, represent windows and window tracery, 5 represent mouldings, and the rest include plan views of piers or responds, doorways, and details of rood screens.

Two passing references to Edward II (Figures 6 and 14), who died in 1327, mark an approximate mid-point for the subject matter discussed. About half the drawings listed belong to the century and a quarter before that date, and another half belong to a longer period after, down to the 1520s in York. Two sites are also mentioned where there are drawings of medieval character from c.1550. Many of the earlier drawings represent geometrical tracery, whereas the later ones are more varied.

Since the purpose of this short book is to look at drawings that have not been adequately described before, the important collection of drawings at York is not further discussed. Recent discoveries in Norfolk are not described either, because they have already been the subject of an energetic programme of publication – references may be found via the gazettteer.

Among problems of interpretation encountered in doing this work, some of the most challenging concern drawings engraved on a stone slab at Gloucester Cathedral. They were mentioned in *Medieval Drawing* in 2007, but their discussion was left on one side at that time. Some analysis is attempted now in Chapter 2, still with only partial success. This is the most involved chapter in the book, and readers new to the subject may find it easiest to postpone reading it to last.

Other chapters describe a number of drawings that have not previously been adequately treated, or which have been discovered recently. Undoubtedly, there are more drawings of these kinds to be found, and one can sometimes anticipate roughly where they might be. For example, in the area where historic Gloucestershire borders Somerset there are many fine medieval buildings. Moreover, when the local stone is dressed, it provides excellent surfaces for drawing. That is demonstrated by the late medieval tithe barn at Englishcombe, Somerset, which once belonged to Bath Abbey. It contains numerous drawings, including circle geometry and drawings of animals and ploughs (some illustrated in *MD*, p 164). But not all are of medieval date and none is connected with architectural design..

Other buildings in the region with drawings on walls include the former chapter house at Hinton Charterhous Priory, Somerset, and the church at Northleach, Gloucestershire. But most of the drawings in these places are small geometrical patterns, and have nothing to do with architecture, and several are post-medieval. Northleach was a "wool church", and some graffiti may be wool merchants' marks. Such examples demonstrate what good drawing surfaces the local stone provided. They also suggest that an important consideration in any survey of mural drawings is to separate medieval from later work, and to distinguish the few examples that have a connection with architectural design from the many that do not.

Arnold Pacey,

Addingham.

March 2015

arnold.pacey@mypostoffice.co.uk

Acknowledgements

In compiling this short book I have been helped especially by Paul Barnwell. Among other things, he visited Gloucester Cathedral on my behalf and made a record of the fireplace overmantel in the Parliament Room, both by taking photographs and by making the rubbings that were essential for an accurately scaled image. I am very appreciative of the time and trouble he took and his many helpful comments since.

The initial edition of *MD* was not well reviewed, so it has been gratifying to hear of postgraduate researchers who have been using it. Some of them have been in touch and have contributed illustrations or information to this work. My gratitude to them is acknowledged in several footnotes and picture credits.

Picture Credits

(Illustrations not credited are the responsibility of the author)

Figure 1   photo: Paul Barnwell

Figure 2   reproduced by permission of the Pepys Library, Magdalene College, Cambridge.

Figure 6   photo: Sophie Dentzer

Figure 7   reproduced with the kind permission of Stuart Harrison. Copyright © Stuart Harrison based on an original photogrammatic drawing by English Heritage.

Figure 9   reproduced by kind permission of D.H. Heslop.

Figure 10   photo and drawing: Ross Lovett

Figure 11   drawing with permission and assistance of John Crook, photo: Philip Pacey.

Figure 13   reproduced with kind permission of John Bailey

Figure 14   photo: Pamela Maryfield

Figure 15   photo: Penny Jones, with kind permission of the Chapter of Wells Cathedral

Figure 16   photo: David Farrar

Abbreviations

The following abbreviations are used in footnotes and the gazetteer:

BAACT   *British Archaeological Association Conference Transactions*

BOE   *Buildings of England* (Pevsner)

JBAA   *Journal of the British Archaeological Association*

MD   *Medieval Architectural Drawing: English Craftsmen's Methods and their Post-medieval Persistence, by Arnold Pacey, Tempus/History Press, 2007.*

RIBA   Royal Institute of British Architects

YAJ   *Yorkshire Archaeological Journal*

CHAPTER 1

What drawings in England?

A book on medieval architectural drawing in Europe discussing examples from all over the continent would have a recognised corpus of some 600 surviving drawings on parchment to consider, with scope for analysis of many detailed aspects of draughtsmanship and design. By contrast, a book on the same subject that confines its view to England has first to establish just what drawings exist, a task whose provisional and incomplete results are summarised in the gazetteer at the end of this publication. There is also a question about which of these drawings can really be accepted as architectural drawings in the sense that they were used in architectural design, or in the training of masons, or as working drawings during construction of buildings. For, in contrast to the numerous well-executed drawings in ink on parchment that exist on the continent dating from the thirteenth century onwards, there is very little on parchment in England, but there are many drawings of a different character on tracing floors and walls.

The subject matter of drawings is different too. Most medieval drawings in England are of details such as windows and mouldings but, according to the best and most recent book on European drawings, the "overwhelming majority" on the continent depict "facades and spires".[1] One famous drawing dating from about 1300 is of the twin-towered west front of Cologne Cathedral. It was drawn on a dozen large sheets of parchment sewn together, plus a few smaller pieces filling gaps, and the drawing as a whole measures just over 4 metres.[2]

To some extent these contrasts between drawings on the continent and in England reflect differences in architecture. Significant numbers of continental drawings show taller, more elaborate elevations than would be usual in England, often with open-work spires, exemplified by the minsters in Ulm and Freiburg, which are of a kind hardly to be seen here. In other words, many continental drawings refer to prestige buildings that made unusual demands on the draughtsman.

---

1   Robert Bork, *The Geometry of Creation*, Farnham: Ashgate 2011, pp. 21, 62.

2   The drawing is held by the Dombauarchiv, Roncalliplatz 2, 50667 Köln, Germany, and is illustrated and analysed by Bork (previous note), pp. 58, 59, 107.

It is also striking that only in a few places were serious efforts made to preserve such drawings, so that 428 out of roughly 600 medieval architectural drawings on parchment in Europe are held in one collection in Vienna.[3] They include drawings connected with cathedrals in Prague, Freiburg, and several other places as well as buildings in Vienna itself.

Drawings of more ordinary buildings were rarely kept, even on the continent. Quite often, the sheets of parchment on which they were drawn were washed clean of ink, cut up into smaller sheets, and used for other purposes. One or two examples of reused parchment with drawing on it can be cited from England, now held in collections at Cambridge and Worcester.[4] That is one reason why so few complete parchment drawings survive. But many drawings were also made on tracing floors which had plaster or stone surfaces, and there are drawings on wooden panels and walls.

Tracing floors had the advantage that drawings could be much larger than was possible even with several sheets of parchment sewn together, and parchment was in any case expensive. In France, tracing floors are known in cathedrals at Clermont-Ferrand (on a flat paved roof),[5] and Soissons (on a stone floor),[6] and in England there are the well-known examples at York Minster and Wells Cathedral,[7] as well as evidence of others elsewhere (such as at Byland Abbey). In addition, there are examples of drawings on plastered walls and on the stonework of piers. Several small drawings are also known that were made on individual blocks of stone, suggesting that craftsmen would sometimes sketch out ideas on the flat surface of a dressed stone while it was still in the masons' yard.

Drawing methods

Before the advent of graphite pencils and erasers that allowed mistakes to be easily removed from a drawing, some draughtsmen did all their initial work with a dry-point or stylus that inscribed lines on the surface of parchment (or plaster, paper or wood) without leaving any ink or other pigment. Such lines were difficult to see, and were only inked in after the draughtsman was satisfied they were correct. Examples on parchment in the Pepys library at Magdalene College, Cambridge, include one which was never inked and so was too faint to illustrate until it was redrawn.[8] Other drawings in the same collection had been inked in, including one represented here in Figure 2. Another example is a sixteenth-century drawing by John Thorpe in which only a few lines had been done in ink, leaving many scribed lines to be found by viewing the drawing in oblique light.[9]

---

3   These drawings are in Kupferstichkabinett der Akademie der bildenden Künste (the Vienna Academy collection).

4   *MD*, pp. 125-6, 139.

5   Michael T. Davis, "On the drawing board", in Nancy Y. Wu (ed.), *Ad Quadratum: the Practical Application of Geometry in Medieval Architecture,* Aldershot: Ashgate, 2002, pp. 183-204.

6   Carl F. Barnes, "The Gothic architectural engravings in the cathedral at Soissons", *Speculum,* 47 (no. 1) 1972.

7   *MD*, pp. 45-58.

8   Pepys Libray, MS. PL 1916, the redrawn version is in *MD*, p. 127.

9   *MD*, p. 182.

The same technique of working with a dry-point, in this case, often a compass point, was used in making drawings on tracing floors, or on walls. What one sees, then, are lines scribed with metal points, sometimes marking plaster or stone surfaces quite heavily. Drawings of this kind are referred to as "engravings" or "inscriptions" by some authors.[10] This is unfortunate because, although the drawings were certainly engraved or inscribed, they should not be made to seem anything other than drawings. They were scribed in just the same way as many drawings on parchment, and were used in designing buildings or communicating designs exactly as any other drawings would be. The only major difference is that they were not portable.

Thus if we are to understand medieval architectural drawings, we have to include those made on stone and plaster surfaces along with those made on parchment, and not just regard them as curiosities. They were scribed with metal points on surfaces of varied type, but most typically on a surface prepared for drawing by applying a skim of plaster or limewash over a stone wall or stone paving or, in some documented examples, wooden boards.[11] The skim would obliterate any earlier drawings, and further applications of plaster would allow the same surface to be used repeatedly. Some drawings, though, were made directly on a dressed stone surface, particularly when it was of a relatively soft stone that was easy to draw on, such as clunch in Cambridgeshire.

The standard drawing instrument was a pair of compasses with metal points on both arms, so when a circle was drawn, with one point held at the centre of the circle, the curve would be inscribed in the plaster or stone by the other point. If pressure was applied, the scribing point could easily penetrate the skim of plaster and mark the underlying stone surface. Later the plaster skim often flaked away leaving an incomplete drawing on the stone, with only the most heavily-drawn curves remaining. An example is in the Galilee Porch at Ely Cathedral, where drawings of the elevation of a building, a window, and several geometrical figures are to be seen, scribed on stonework to which some areas of plaster still adhere.[12]

Another example of drawings on a plaster-skimmed stone surface is in former monastic buildings attached to Gloucester Cathedral (a former abbey), in what is known as the Parliament Room. Here there is a fifteenth-century fireplace with a plain overmantel or lintel consisting of a large limestone slab, 160 mm thick (cover photograph) with some plaster attached. The slab was once used as what has been described as a "mason's setting-out table".[13] On it can be seen outlines of shaped profiles and compass-drawn circles. Inscribed particularly emphatically is a grid of lines similar to those on the tracing floors at Wells and York, but more tightly meshed (Figure 1, where letters A-D identify particular curves that will be explained in the next chapter).

---

10   Peter Fergusson, "Notes on two Cistercian engraved designs", *Speculum*, 54, 1979, pp. 1-17.

11   Whitewashed or limewashed boards were also used by stained-glass artists for drawing out their cartoons.

12   *MD*, pp. 33-4, 38.

13   David Verey and Alan Brooks, *BOE Gloucestershire, 2: The Vale and the Forest of Dean*, Yale University Press, 2002, p. 432. I am indebted to Paul Barnwell for photographs, rubbings and notes on the overmantel, and to Kirsty Rodwell for her comments.

Figure 1

Detail of drawings on the fireplace slab at Gloucester, with an ogee curve at A and bowtells in two places marked B, and other shapes explained in Chapter 2.

(photo: Paul Barnwell)

The slab is an important survival, and appears to have been moved to its present position above the fireplace after 1400, which is after it had ceased to be used as a drawing surface. Since it is known that there were tracing floors paved in stone in other places, for example, at Ely and Byland Abbey, the question arises whether this large slab was ever part of such a floor. The drawings on it seem relatively small and there is no sign of large drawings of window tracery such as are seen on the tracing floors at Wells and York.

The slab has been trimmed to fit the shape needed for the fireplace, but is probably not much smaller than in its previous use, when it may well, as suggested, have been a horizontal table reserved for drawing smaller items. Perhaps it was located in a workshop that specialised in cutting mouldings for arches, plinths, string courses, mullions and the like. It was evidently used many times to make drawings, and seems to have been given a skim of plaster or limewash when a new drawing was started to provide a clean surface with no distracting lines showing from earlier work. Most, but not all, this plaster has now flaked away but, because the base-lines and centre-lines of drawings were scored more heavily than the architectural subject matter, they were cut through the plaster into the stone below and comprise most of what now remains.

Drawn profiles of mouldings

Apart from the emphatic grid illustrated in Figure 1, there are superimposed fragments of several drawings, some of which can be recognised as profiles (or outlines) of mouldings. Before attempting to analyse the latter, it may be worth noting the conventions used in representing mouldings and the nomenclature employed to describe them. A good place to start is an occasion in the fifteenth century when a scholar and clerk William Worcestre (1415-85) visited Bristol and encountered a mason named Benedict Crosse working at St Stephen's Church. Crosse drew out for Worcestre, on the paper of a page of the latter's notebook, a section through a moulding on the jambs of the church doorway.[14] He then named different parts of the moulding, using terms such as "bowtell" and "casement", which Worcestre duly noted down.

An earlier example of the same style of drawing is one of very few English architectural drawings on parchment surviving from before 1400. It is in a sketch-book or "model book" preserved in Cambridge and was quoted earlier because of a drawing it includes that was scribed with a stylus and never inked in. The sketchbook was put together in the fourteenth century but later belonged to Samuel Pepys.[15]

One drawing in the book, finished in ink, has moulding profiles represented by lines and curves without shading or hatching. It has no annotations to name parts of the moulding or to show whether it is to be understood solely as a model, or whether it belonged to a specific building, but a number of curves regularly used in buildings have been marked with letters in Figure 2, where they are identified using terminology that Benedict Crosse might have employed.

---

14   Notebook held by Corpus Christi College, Cambridge, and illustrated in *MD*, Plates 11 and 12; pp. 120-1.

15   MS. PL 1916, Pepys Library, Magdalene College, Cambridge.

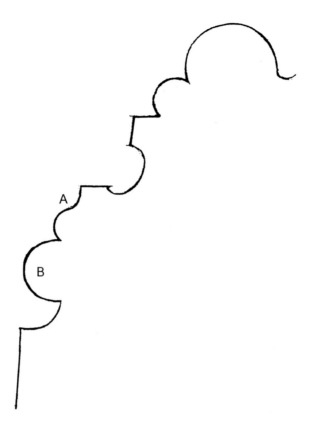

Figure 2

One of two drawings for mouldings from the fourteenth-century sketch-book in the Pepys Library, Magdalene College, Cambridge. This profile includes an ogee curve (A), and a bowtell (B), both shapes also to be seen in Figure 1 identified by the same letters. The original also includes a faint palimpsest drawing.

(Reproduced by kind permission of the Pepys Library, Magdalene College.)

CHAPTER 2

Drawings on the Gloucester overmantel

The sketch-book drawing of a moulding profile illustrated in Figure 2 is a good preparation for examining drawings on the overmantel slab at Gloucester which include several more mouldings. This similarity in subject matter, and the terminology used by the mason Benedict Crosse, should mean that some drawings on the slab make more sense than they do at first glance. Figures 1 and 3 illustrate part of the fireplace overmantel by means of a photograph and a diagram. A particularly useful analysis of some of the details that show in these illustrations has been provided by Rose Harris-Adamson.[16] Among the lines and curves, apart from the irregular grid of straight lines, there is a series of curves to be seen above what is now the left-hand end of the fireplace and they are marked by letters B, D, C, B and A, running down the page in Figure 3.

The latter illustration provides a diagrammatic method of analysing these curves, together with others extending to near the fireplace opening. Below the upper group of shapes labelled BDCBA there is a longer sequence running from A to CDB and then CDB again This continues downward to what is now the the corner of the fireplace opening (Figure 3). Harris-Adamson interprets this sequence, over 30 cm long from A through the repetition of CDB, as representing a single, complex moulding, although close inspection reveals some small breaks in continuity that may (or may not) be significant.

Assuming that the second, longer sequence of curves is indeed all a single drawing, we may think it represents detail of a richly-moulded doorway opening or arch. Comprehensive studies of medieval mouldings such these have been made by Richard K. Morris.[17]

---

16   Rose Harris-Adamson, "Stone masons' drawings on building fabric", *Archaeological Journal, 171*, 2014, pp. 258-88.

17   R.K. Morris, "The development of later Gothic mouldings in England, c.1250-1400", *Architectural History*, 22, 1979, pp. 21-57.

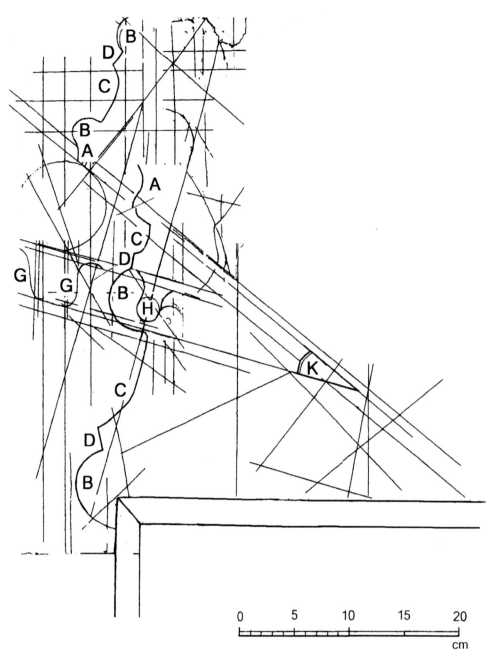

Figure 3

*Diagram showing curves at the left-hand end of the Gloucester overmantel,
with many background lines suppressed. Letters identify specific types of
curve with the sequence BDCBA at the top also shown in Figure 1.*

Using Morris's information, Harris-Adamson has identified this long moulding profile as an ogee-bowtell moulding such as occurs in the south transept of the former abbey church – the present Gloucester Cathedral – where it was introduced about 1337.[18]

18   Rose Harris-Adamson, as note 16.

This, of course, is the kind of terminology used by Benedict Crosse, the Bristol mason. For example, what he called a bowtell (with variable spelling) is a plain round moulding, marked B in Figures 1 – 3 each time it occurs. On the other hand, the term fillet (for Crosse) refers to almost any flat surface that comes to a sharp corner or edge, and is marked here as D. Another type of curve is a reverse curve or ogee, labelled A in Figures 1- 3. Crosse called this a "ressant".

Also to be seen on the slab is a hollow curve such as Crosse would have called a casement (C). This occurs at three places in Figure 3, usually with a fillet (D) adjoining it. Often, indeed, a fillet intervenes between a casement (C) and a bowtell (B). These shapes are perhaps more clearly seen in Figure 4, which is a sketch indicating how they might look in three dimensions when cut in stone.

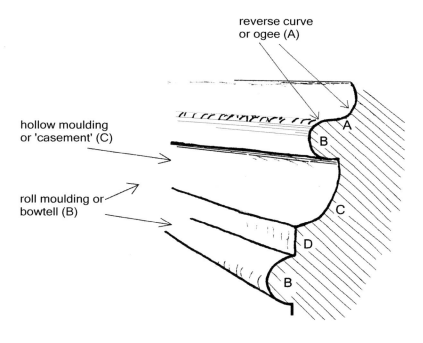

Figure 4

Perspective sketch of mouldings with profiles A-D

Design for vaults?

One difficulty about interpreting lines and curves on the slab is that so many drawings are superimposed. The long ogee-bowtell profile running down the slab from A near the top to near the corner of the fireplace opening is crossed at H by a different drawing which slopes down from the horizontal on an alignment G, H, K (Figure 3).

The main feature of this drawing is a series of sloping parallel lines. There are also curves that apparently make links between these lines. Included among them are reverse curves (or ogee curves) in the two places marked G. Most striking of all is a small circle at H that is linked to the sloping lines by short arcs (Figure 3, at G-G and H). The sloping line to which circle H is attached extends to the right to meet another sloping line at K, making an angle of approximately 23 degrees.

An attempt at interpreting this might begin by noting that when straight lines on medieval drawings are inclined to one another at sharp angles that do not fit the grid of perpendiculars, they sometimes represent a plan view of vaulting ribs. An example is a drawing on the Wells tracing floor that has been identified as representing ribs in the vault above cloister walks at Wells.[19]

So a hypothesis about the inclined lines on the slab at Gloucester, especially along the alignment G – K, is that they are paired to represent the widths of vaulting ribs and have curves associated with them to represent the profiles of the mouldings on the ribs. Thus the detail at G and H may represent rib profiles, the rib itself being represented by the parallel lines on either side. At G, the drawing is incomplete, but at H a rib of rounded profile seems to be implied.

Above the cloister walks at Gloucester is a vaulted ceiling of complex design in which some ribs are aligned at 22½ degrees to one another (although they are interrupted before they actually converge). They have a more rounded section than most ribs in the cathedral, though not as markedly rounded as suggested by the drawn circle at H. The cloister vault as a whole is far more complicated than anything drawn on the slab, but the drawing could have been intended only for shapes of rib profiles to be worked out.

Identification of drawing GHK with the cloister vault makes a good deal of sense but the drawings are not complete enough for this to be more than an informed guess. Much the same uncertainty surrounds other drawings, notably those to the right of the crack which runs up the centre of the slab. Here are two circular forms that are illustrated in Figure 5, labelled M and N. Also of interest to the left of the crack are less clearly defined details at P and R in the same illustration.

The incomplete circle labelled M is particularly striking, and could represent another bowtell moulding, but a straight line is drawn through its centre and is perpendicular to another straight line tangential to it. The tangent is one of another series of inclined lines that again suggest a vault rib, and the relationship of these lines to circle M can be compared with the relationship of inclined lines discussed earlier to circle H, except that the spacing of the inclined parallel lines and the radius of the circle is larger here.

Also to be seen in Figure 5 is a complete circle of 9 cm diameter marked N, with several radius lines marked like spokes and a well-worn centre point. Harris-Adamson suggests that the diameter of this circle was a standard dimension, marked here for reference.[20]

Other drawings are at P and R. The first shows the section of what looks like a very slender mullion with ogee profiled sides. If this is a full-size drawing, it is too small to be a window mullion, but could be a fine detail from a funerary monument. There are several in the cathedral that could be relevant, the most famous commemorating Edward II, who was buried here after his death in 1327. His tomb, probably made in the 1330s, has a remarkable vaulted canopy, made of oolitic

---

19   *MD*, pp. 68-70.

20   Rose Harris-Adamson, as note 16, pp. 266-7

limestone (Figure 6). But even though the ribs of this vault are of unusually small dimensions, they are significantly bigger than what is indicated in the drawing, and do not have the same ogee profile. In detail, the rib profiles in the canopy are not quite consistent everywhere because, in places, the ribs serve to hide slender rectangular iron bars that tie the canopy together. All this makes it seem that the drawing marked P in Figure 5 is smaller than anything actually constructed, so is probably to be interpreted as a sketch rather than a full-size drawing.

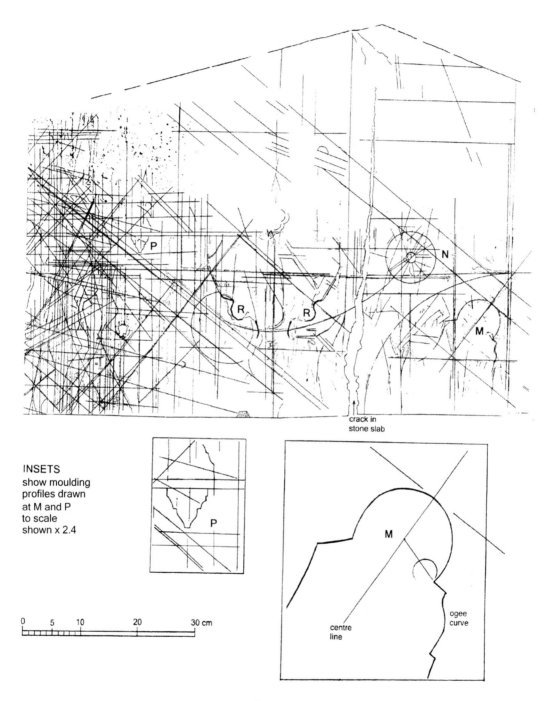

Figure 5

Detail from the inscribed drawings in the Parliament Room at Gloucester

As for the curves drawn on the slab at R and R', their irregularity may be due to scratches and other damage to the slab, or to the uneven survival of detail after plaster flaked away. However, the shapes drawn at R and R' look almost as if they are two halves of a symmetrical shape, possibly a large, elaborately moulded mullion.

To sum up, the architectural drawings on the fireplace overmantel at Gloucester, apart from the array of straight lines forming overlapping grids, mostly appear to be connected with mouldings and vaults. Profiles of mouldings that may have been intended to enrich arches or doorway openings are represented by various combination of shapes A to D on the left of the slab. It seems likely that they are designs connected with work in the south transept of the cathedral dating from 1330 and are connected with the early Perpendicular phases of the cathedral – the former abbey church.

Less certain is the identification of the sloping parallel lines as vault ribs, and curves such as those at H and M as incomplete drawings of mouldings on the ribs. No vault is drawn out fully, but enough of several ribs is shown for a mason to work out the size and profile of the ribs.

Figure 6

Vaulted canopy over the tomb of Edward II in Gloucester Cathedral.

(Photo: Sophie Dentzer)

CHAPTER 3

Drawings at Yorkshire monasteries

Much earlier than the drawings at Gloucester are incised lines and curves dating from close to 1200 at Byland Abbey in the (former) North Riding of Yorkshire. There were two drawings here, both showing parts of the great rose window that once filled the west front of the abbey church, but while one was on a tracing floor, now destroyed, another is located inside the west wall of the church, below where the rose window was installed. This drawing shows a rosette with six lobes, in other words a sexfoil, and is probably a full-size representation of the central feature of the window.[21] Photographs show that, despite weathering and lichen growth, the outer curve of the rosette drawing can still be seen on the wall to the right of the middle doorway.[22]

Several component parts of the rose window's stonework have been identified among fallen masonry, making it possible for Stuart Harrison to produce a reconstruction of the whole window and fit it to an accurate drawing of the west front (Figure 7).[23]

With regard to the purposes for which the drawings at Byland were made, full-size outlines such as were formerly on the tracing floor above the warming house would be needed to make templates, that is, flat wooden patterns (often of beech or oak) for the shapes the masons had to cut in stone.[24] By contrast, the drawing on the west wall of the church shows detail of the centre of the window which was probably also shown on the tracing floor. But a drawing on a wall would have been no good for making templates, because they usually needed to be laid out flat.

---

21 Stuart Harrison and Paul Barker, "Byland Abbey...the west front and rose window reconstructed", *JBAA*, 140, 1987, pp. 134-151.

22 Photographs have been published by Harrison and Barker, previous note, and in *MD*, plates 19 and 20.

23 Harrison and Barker, as note 21. The date usually given for the west front of the abbey is in the 1190s, but the impression can be gained that the rose window itself is slightly later.

24 John Harvey, *Medieval Craftsmen*, London: Batsford, 1975, p. 120.

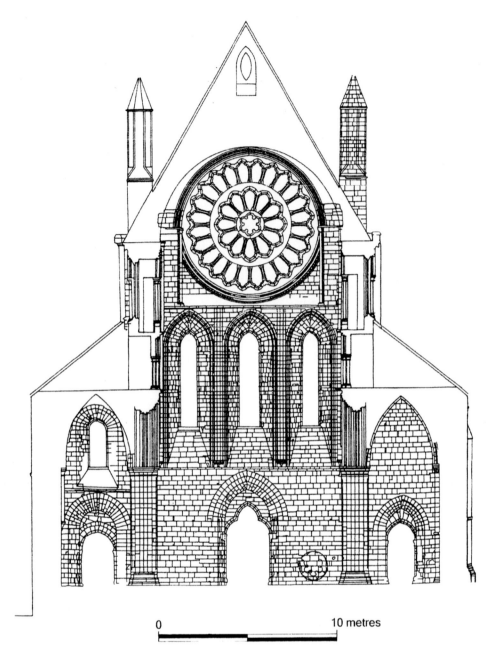

Figure 7

*Byland Abbey: internal elevation of the west front with a reconstruction
of the rose window by Stuart Harrison. A full-size drawing of the central
sexfoil opening in the window can be seen in this illustration inscribed on
the wall to the right of the middle doorway.*

(by kind permission of Stuart Harrison. Copyright © Stuart Harrison, based on an original
photogrammetric drawing by English Heritage)

What is significant, though, is that the rose window to which the drawings refer was located
in the west wall immediately above the mural drawing. For although, in principle, drawings on
walls could be used for working out details of a design, this is one of several examples which are
so near the part of the building to which they refer that it seems likely that their function was to

be consulted during construction. Another example where a drawing relevant to a west window in a monastic church is on the wall immediately inside the west wall is Binham Priory, Norfolk.[25]

Another Cistercian house, 24 miles west of Byland and with close links to it, was Jervaulx Abbey in Wensleydale. This may once have had a large rose window as well but, although there are substantial standing walls remaining of its dormitory and related structures, the abbey church has little standing higher than the plinths and bases of piers and walls. On looking at these and at some of the loose stone on the site, occasional examples of setting-out lines and assembly marks can be found including cross-shaped marks on cut stones that were probably part of ribs in an aisle vault. They are similar to the assembly marks on vaulting bosses from St Mary's Abbey, York.[26]

When the base of the east wall of the presbytery at Jervaulx is examined, projections are seen in the foundation where the north and south arcades terminated in responds. Each of the latter has a plinth in the shape of half an octagon supporting the base of the respond, whose mouldings show that it had five attached shafts. The upper courses of masonry have gone from both the wall and the respond leaving a flat surface on the lowest remaining course of stonework. This flat area has several curves scribed on it to represent the shafts on the respond (Figure 8). Peter Fergusson argues that they were used for making the templates employed in cutting stone for construction of the shafts.[27] He also compares the rosette drawing on the west wall at Byland, which he seems to have misunderstood.

In other buildings where stonework has been dismantled, or where construction was left incomplete, it is quite common to see setting-out lines and curves marking the intended position of the next stones to be laid. At Jervaulx, whatever the role of these curves in the production of templates, they were primarily guide-lines of this kind. An example of the same thing, quoted by Robert Branner, is what he called "stencils" for the springing of a vault inscribed on stone in Southwark Cathedral, London.[28] These turn out to be setting-out lines and curves, marked on stone to guide placing of stone components of the vault. They are not design drawings.

Another example is in Ripon Cathedral where a planned replacement for one of the crossing arches was never built. But on the flat top of the pier that was to have supported it, "there is engraved a plan of exactly how stones were to be assembled to support the new pointed arch", including a detailed profile of mouldings.[29] What is different at Jervaulx, by comparison, is that an alternative design was indicated – a design which seems to have been made before the respond base was cut to its present dimensions. Hence this is not solely a setting-out drawing, but records a stage in the development of the design as well.

---

25   Matthew Champion, "Tracery designs at Binham Priory", *English Heritage Historical Review*, 6, 2011, pp. 2-16.

26   *MD*, Plate 4.

27   Peter Fergusson, "Notes on two Cistercian engraved designs", *Speculum*, 54, 1979, pp. 1-17.

28   Robert Branner, quoting Robert Willis. In Lynn T. Courtenay (ed.), *The Engineering of Medieval Cathedrals*, Aldershot: Ashgate, 1997, p. 67.

29   Bill Forster, Bill Robson and Jennifer Deadman, *Ripon Cathedral: its History and Architecture*, York: William Sessions, 1993, p. 89. The location of this drawing is totally inaccessible except when scaffolding is erected.

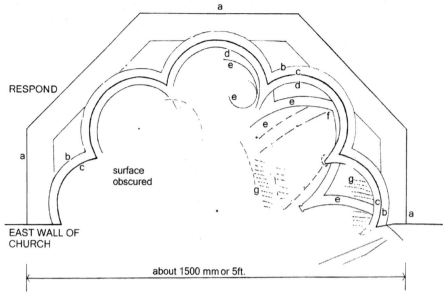

RESPOND

a

d
e

b
c
d

e

e
e

f

surface
obscured

g
g

e

c
b
a

EAST WALL OF
CHURCH

about 1500 mm or 5ft.

Figure 8

Jervaulx Abbey, North Riding of Yorkshire: plan view of a respond in the east wall of the church with drawing on horizontal stonework exposed by post-dissolution demolition.

Key:

a   *semi-octagonal base of respond.*

b   *moulding.*

c   *heavy line showing edge of surface used for drawing.*

d   *scribed curves where cut stones forming the five-shafted shape of the respond were to be placed.*

e   *scribed curves of earlier drawing.*

f   *outline of keeled shaft.*

g   *tooling on axe-dressed surface.*

Also in the North Riding of Yorkshire, but nearer the coast and the estuary of the River Tees was the Augustinian priory at Gisborough (or Guisborough). Here, archaeologists have found incised drawings on paved floors below where the westernmost arches of the nave once stood on both north and south sides of the nave.

On the north side there are three separate drawings, one being a group of three circles, another showing concentric circles and a third a design for a gabled ornament. The drawing from the south side of the nave was interpreted by the archaeologist responsible for its discovery, David Heslop, as the plan view of a wall pier.[30] Initially it was thought that the design might refer to the masonry between two clerestory windows since it includes two rebated window jambs, one on each side (Figure 9, d and d'). A later view is that this may have been part of a design for the west front of the priory church where, above the west doors, there was probably a row of lancets with piers of this pattern between them.[31]

30   D.H. Heslop, "Excavation within the church at the Augustinian priory of Gisborough, Cleveland, 1985-6", *Yorkshire Archaeological Journal*, 67, 1995, pp. 51-74.

31   Stuart A. Harrison and D.H. Heslop, "Archaeological survey of the Augustinian priory of Gisborough", *Yorkshire Archaeological Journal*, 71, 1999, pp. 89-127.

A difficulty with this or any other interpretation is that the only part of Gisborough Priory that still stands is the east wall of the church, a noble structure with the large arched opening for a spectacular east window. However, study of fallen masonry in the "stone pile" on site has allowed archaeologists to deduce a good deal about the lost architecture of the church, including lancets in the west front, and a rose window above them that was somewhat larger than the one which once existed at Byland Abbey.[32]

There is a degree of complexity about the drawing in Figure 9 which may indicate that alternative designs were being considered. The masonry between the two window jambs is shown as having quite complex mouldings (marked b, a and b'), but in practice these would be obscured by the attached shafts (marked c). Hence it seems possible that the original design did not include the shafts at c, which may have been added as a modification to what was at first planned to be a rather austere elevation.

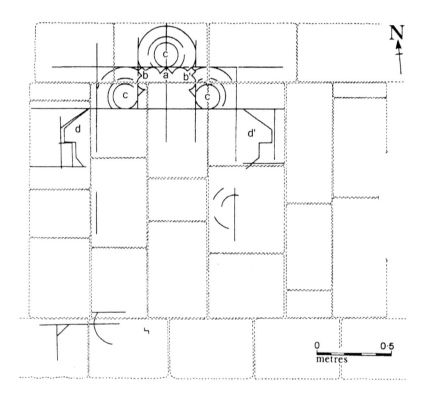

Figure 9

Gisborough Priory: paved floor on the south side of the nave with joints between paving stones shown as dashed lines and a drawing interpreted as the plan view of a wall pier.

This has a right-angled rib (a) on its north side and flat filleted roll mouldings to east and west of the rib (b, b'). Associated with the pier are three shafts of circular section (c), and there are two rebated window jambs, one on each side (d, d').

(Reproduced with kind permission from D.H. Heslop, "Excavations within the church of the Augustinian priory at Gisborough, Cleveland, 1985-6", *YAJ*, 67, 1995, pp. 51-74.)

---

32   Ibid; also D.H. Heslop, as note 30, p. 68.

Referring to these drawings at Gisborough Priory and the fact that they are on a church floor, Harris-Adamson makes the point that this may have been typical of the way tracing floors were contrived in buildings under construction. It would probably be more common to make temporary use of a floor in the building itself rather than creating more permanent, purpose-built tracing floors such as those at Wells and York.[33] Drawings on walls usually had different functions and the same author illustrates one in Salisbury Cathedral, on the south wall of the nave south aisle, which she classes as a presentation drawing rather than a working drawing. What remains is fragmentary, but it can be reliably reconstructed from its 5-metre-long base line as representing a pair of two-light windows very similar to some in the cathedral's north porch.[34]

As regards the full-size outline drawings at Byland, Jervaulx and Gisborough, they illustrate three kinds of location where drawings were sometimes made – on walls, on floors, and on top of stonework where further stones were to be laid. They also illustrate several different functions that a medieval architectural drawing could have – it could be part of the design process, or used for making templates, or for builders to consult while laying stone, or to guide positioning of cut stones when they were being laid in a wall or fitted in an arch or vault.

---

33   Rose Harris-Adamson, "Stonemasons' drawings on building fabric", *Archaeological Journal*, 171, 2014, pp. 258-88.

34   Ibid, pp. 281-5.

CHAPTER 4

Hampshire drawings

There are are three sites in Hampshire where drawings on walls have been recorded and, in each case, they seem to be drawings made as part of a design process rather than for any of the other functions mentioned in the previous chapter. One of these, in St Mary's Church at Old Basing, is relatively late in date, and will not be discussed here in any detail.[35]

The second example is at Christchurch Priory, and the third in Winchester Cathedral. The latter is a drawn quatrefoil below where the north wall of the retrochoir has a series of blind quatrefoils framed by mouldings. This decorative work is above a wall arcade and just above window-sill level, on a parapet where a wall passage crosses the window openings. Below these, framed by an arch in the wall arcade, is the drawing.[36] It represents a differently oriented quatrefoil compared with those carved on the parapet above, and has groups of small circles on each side that could be suggestions for additional decoration (Figure 10, top).

The drawing may be a preliminary design for the blind quatrefoils, made when a completely different version of these details was being considered, so it is interpreted as a design drawing throughout this book. Caution is needed, though, because elsewhere in the cathedral there are drawings of a different kind scribed on walls. They include circle patterns that have nothing to do with architecture or design, but may have had a ritual purpose. The suggestion can be made that some time *after* the blind quatrefoils on this wall had been completed, people such as those responsible for the other circle patterns set out the quatrefoil drawings as a response to the architecture.

---

35 John Crook' "New light on the history of St. Mary's Church, Old Basing, Hampshire: an incised design", JBAA, 154, 2001, pp. 92-132

36 I am ndebted to Maud Hurley for alerting me to this drawing and to Ross Lovett for help in developing an accurate copy of it.

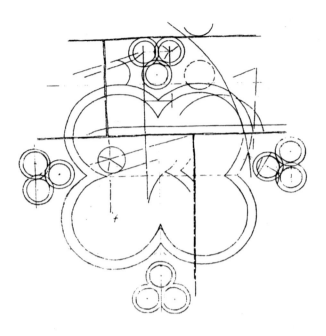

Figure 10

*Drawing on the north wall of the retrochoir in Winchester Cathedral
(above) with red arrow (below) showing the position of the drawing relative
to the wall arcade. Note the series of blank quatrefoils in the wall above.
(photo and help with drawing: Ross Lovett)*

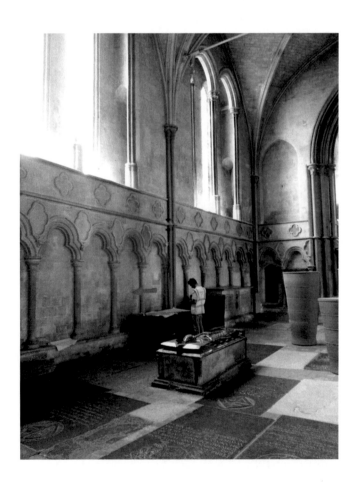

That seems unlikely, because this is a design that a draughtsman has taken trouble with, not a casual sketch, but there is nothing to establish its date with certainty, and it may be that it is later than the wall arcade and the quatrefoil scheme rather than something drafted out in advance of construction.

Figure 10 includes a photograph in which the blank quatrefoils can be seen above the wall arcade, together with an arrow identifying the site of the drawing, a copy of which is shown in the same illustration. The copy is not precisely to scale, but the whole drawing occupies a space 600 mm (about 2 ft) square and overlaps joints between blocks of stone (joints are marked as double lines). Apart from the quatrefoil in the drawing and its triplets of circles, there are some construction lines in the drawing, and curves surviving from an earlier version of the drawing.

A mural drawing which is certainly a preliminary design rather than a sketch made afterwards or a working drawing is at Christchurch Priory, Hampshire (now Dorset). Somewhat more than 2 metres wide and probably intended to be full size, this damaged and now incomplete drawing is on a plastered wall in an upper-floor room. It has been recorded by John Crook and shows a circle in the head of a pointed window, with a six-lobed (or sexfoil) pattern drawn within it (Figure 11). The six lobes were themselves drawn as small circles, as can be seen from holes in the plastered wall surface where the compass point was placed to draw each one.[37] Below the sexfoil circle was a fragment from another circle on the left, this time originally with five lobes, indicating a cinquefoil opening. The drawing was probably symmetrical with another cinquefoil on the other side.

The upper-floor room in which the drawing is located is reached via a stone spiral stair rising from the north-east corner of the north transept. One account of Christchurch Priory refers to it as the "tracing room",[38] presumably because of the drawing, but it is now the boiler room and houses the heating plant and an electricity switchboard. The latter partly obscures the drawing which, in this context, has become a somewhat sorry sight.

---

37   For John Crook's description and discussion, see the notes on Christchurch in his discussion of St. Mary's Church, Old Basing, as in note 35 above, especially p. 129.

38   Benjamin Polk, *Christchurch Priory*, London: Academy Editions, 1994, p. 46; I am indebted to Len Wigg of Christchurch and to my brother, Philip Pacey, for information on the tracing room/boiler room.

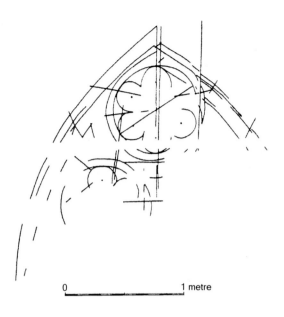

0 _____ 1 metre

Figure 11

*Christchurch Priory: mural drawing in a chamber above the Montacute
Chapel apparently referring to the window in that chapel, illustrated below.*

(Drawing recorded by John Crook; photo: Philip Pacey)

This part of the building was the site of a twelfth-century apsed transept chapel that was altered at some time around the 1260s to 1280s to create a chantry chapel of rectangular plan – the Montacute Chapel. What is now the first-floor boiler room was then a chamber immediately above the new chapel, and the drawing was made on a wall in this space, presumably during the process of designing tracery for the window in the chapel below.

The main difference between the drawing and the window as executed (photograph in Figure 11) is that, instead of having a sexfoil circle above two slightly smaller cinquefoils, the topmost opening in the actual window is a cinquefoil of the same diameter as the ones below. Thus three cinquefoilds of the same size make the head of the completed window narrower and more compact than in the drawing, fitting it under the more steeply pointed arch in the photograph.

There are no documented dates for this work, nor is the sequence in which alterations were made at Christchurch entirely clear. However, it seems that, a little earlier, the windows of the north aisle of the nave had been replaced by the modest, two-light windows that now exist, and although they do not have elaborate tracery, the apex of each one is a cinquefoil of much the same kind as in the Montacute chantry chapel window.

It is tempting to think that the drawing in the present boiler room was drafted out by the mason who had previously made the new windows for the north aisle, and that he was working out how to use similar details in the bigger window required for the Montacute chapel. But the space available in the chapel was rather cramped, being hemmed in by remaining twelfth-century masonry. The drawing shows a wider window than was actually constructed, so it seems that, after making the drawing, the mason had to modify the design and make a narrower window with a smaller apex circle with cinquefoil cusping. The Montacute chapel must have been almost complete at this stage, but without its east window.

It seems, then that the drawing represents a stage in the design of the window, before a final decision had been made as to the precise width. The drawings at Winchester and Old Basing also seem to be design drawings, even though the design process cannot be so easily followed at these sites.

CHAPTER 5

Small drawings for design, geometry and memory

The drawings illustrated from Christchurch and Winchester both differ from what was executed in ways which suggest that, although they were not the final design for what was to be built, they represent a fairly advanced stage in the design process. By comparison, Figure 12 illustrates three drawings of about the same period scribed on walls which are not completed designs in any sense. They are smaller, rougher, and more like sketches. All have been redrawn here to a common format, each one with a scale so that the size of the original can be checked. Some missing lines have been interpolated as dashed lines. The three images together show the considerable variety in geometrical tracery designs for which there are drawings. Although each one has a circle at the apex with varying numbers of cusps, in other ways they differ considerably.

The example from Cambridge was published by Coulton in the 1920s and shows a late thirteenth-century design that was inscribed on a slab of stone (or, more specifically, clunch).[39] It was found at St. John's College, incorporated within the fabric of a wall.[40] The drawing is very small – it does not extend over the whole slab and measures only 14.5 x 9 cm. It represents only half the width of the window. For the purposes of Figure 12, the other half is shown by dashed lines. The circle at the top of the window was intended to have five lobes, and so can be described as a cinquefoil. Below it, two circles were intended, one of which contains arcs that appear to be the first stage in drawing a trefoil. All this is supported by three arch shapes, each with a conventional quatrefoil at its head.

The geometry in the Cambridge drawing consists mainly of arcs of circles, and is accurately set out. Some commentators find it just as impressive as the large drawings on tracing floors because of the way it shows craftsmen working with precision on whatever surfaces came to hand, perhaps to explore the principle of a new design, or perhaps to instruct apprentice masons.[41] Also

---

39   G.G. Coulton, *Art and the Reformation*, Oxford: Blackwell, 1928, p. 178.

40   The illustration in Figure 12 is based on Coulton's published version. See also Malcolm Hislop, *Medieval Masons*, Princes Risborough: Shire, 2000, p. 22 The stone slab is now in the University of Cambridge Museum of Archeology and Anthropology.

41   Anthony Gerbino and Stephen Johnston, *Compass and Rule: Architecture as Mathematical Practice in England*, Yale University Press, 2009, p.39.

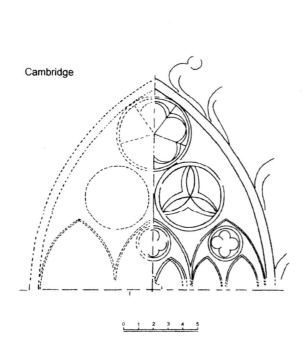

Cambridge

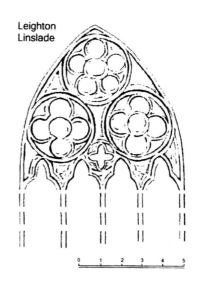

Leighton
Linslade

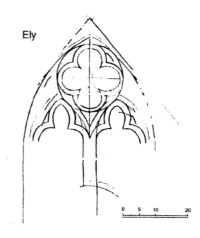

Ely

Figure 12

*Three thirteenth-century drawings of geometrical tracery on stone or
plaster, redrawn to comparable formats. The original drawings vary
greatly in size as shown by the scales of centimetres, but none is near full
size. Dashed lines show interpolations.*

Cambridge: *drawing on stone from St John's College, now in University
Museum of Archaeology and Anthropolgy, illustrated by G.G. Coulton, 1928.*

Leighton Linslade, *Bedfordshire, drawing on wall of church, recorded
by Reginald Hine c.1930 and by Pacey 1981; also illustrated by Pevsner,
Buildings of England, 1968.*

Ely Cathedral, *drawing on wall of Galilee porch, recorded by Violet
Pritchard, 1967, and by Pacey, 2002.*

25

included in this conspectus of drawings of geometrical windows is a small, roughly-drawn sketch on the wall of the church of Leighton Linslade, Bedfordshire (part of Leighton Buzzard). This sketch is now well-known, having been illustrated by Pevsner,[42] though the illustration in Figure 12 was recorded on site by the author.[43] It shows a window head with a cinquefoil circle at the top, two quatrefoiles below, then a single, small quatrefoil punctuating the centre of a row of arches. While the circles in this drawing have been accurately drawn with compasses, the straight lines representing mullions were very roughly sketched in, and are shown by dashed lines here.

These drawings are comparable with one in the Galilee porch at Ely Cathedral that forms part of a group of drawings previously mentioned. It is a simple two-light window, as shown at bottom right in Figure 12 with just one circle at its head. Maddison suggests that this may refer to a window actually inserted into the south transept about 1250, and thinks that there may also have been a larger drawing on a floor, perhaps with the Galilee Porch in temporary use as a tracing house. This would have been more than a century earlier than the documentary evidence for a stone-paved tracing floor at Ely.[44]

Tracery drawn on detached stone blocks

Although the drawing from Cambridge is on a slab which was at one time incorporated in a wall, it is likely that the drawing was made before that, when the stone was lying in the masons' yard. Drawings made on detached slabs or blocks of stone that were later built into walls or other structures can be cited from several sites, including Lincoln. There may also be an instance at Canterbury Cathedral, where the top step in the north stair of the Corona tower is inscribed with the outline of a window design.[45] This may be a piece of stone inserted during repairs that had previously been used for a drawing in the masons' yard, or it may be that the top of the Corona was used by masons as a secluded place for working out designs. As with the examples in Figure 12, this scribed drawing is of geometrical tracery, but surmounted by emphatically-drawn crockets. The tracery includes two pairs of pointed lights each supporting a compass-drawn circle and there are more circles in the apex.[46] The crockets suggest an early fourteenth-century design, which makes it much later than the twelfth-century structure of the Corona in which it is set.

Yet another drawing that seems to have been made on a detached block, rather than on a completed wall, is in Holy Trinity Church at Dartford, Kent, and has been illustrated and described by John Bailey.[47] It comprises quite a small sketch of an elaborate tracery design incised on stone high in a

---

42   Nikolaus Pevsner, *BOE Bedfordshire, Huntingdon and Peterborough*, Penguin, 1968, p.108.

43   The drawing was also recorded by Reginald Hine in the 1920s; see "Collections of graffiti in English churches compiled by Reginald Hine, FSA", Society of Antiquaries, London, boxes numbered 788/1-3.

44   John Maddison, *Ely Cathedral: Design and Meaning*, Ely Cathedral Publications, 2000, pp. 56-7.

45   This drawings should not be confused with scribed marks recently discovered by the Canterbury Archaeological Trust in chambers under the Corona staircases, which are really masons' marks of unusual form (see the Trust's website).

46   A photograph with interpretation is provided by Toby Huitson, *Stairway to Heaven: the Function of Medieval Upper Spaces*, Oxford: Oxbow Books, 2014, p. 135.

47   The tracing was made by Howard Jones and was published by John Bailey in *Church Archaeology*, vol. 1, March 1997, pp. 46-7.

wall. The sketch is approximately 17cm in width and was made on a single block of Reigate stone before the block was set in the wall. That is clear because the stone was laid so that the drawing now appears upside down. Figure 13 is a tracing of this drawing and shows a four-light window design with a large central quatrefoil at the apex. The drawing was accurately set out with metal dividers serving as compasses, and the centre points of some circles can be seen as small holes or pricks left by the compass point in the stone surface.

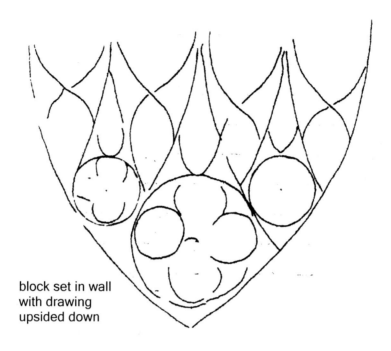

block set in wall
with drawing
upsided down

Figure 13

Drawing in Holy Trinity Church, Dartford, Kent

(by kind permission of John Bailey).

Interpretation of the drawing is not straightforward because, although the circles and quatrefoils in the head of the window indicate the geometrical style, there are also curves that suggest curvilinear tracery. Motifs of these different kinds are not usually combined, but John Bailey cites the Lady Chapel east window in Exeter Cathedral and windows in Merton College chapel, Oxford, as having similar combinations of forms.[48] Both these are "late geometrical", and there is documentary evidence for alterations to the church at Dartford early in the fourteenth century that may have included windows of this kind.

Questions arise as to the function of drawings such as these which are so much smaller than working drawings or *épures*. One might even think that they are smaller than a draughtsman would choose for any serious work. Yet in the Cambridge drawing in Figure 12, the geometry of the design is represented very precisely. A suggestion that might be relevant is made by Michael Davis in discussing drawings of window tracery at Clermont Cathedral (Clermont-Ferrand, France). He suggests that masons used "visual mnemonics" to help them remember geometrical

---

48   Ibid.

procedures for constructing complicated designs.[49] It seems possible that some small drawings – those that are especially precise geometrically – may have functioned as mnemonics in this sense. They would have been something that was easy for somebody with a background in medieval geometry to remember.

A different but related suggestion refers to a small but neat drawing of this kind at Weston Longville near Norwich,[50] which has been recorded by the Norfolk Medieval Graffiti Survey.[51] Laurie Smith says that such images on church walls, "are clearly drawn as explanatory geometries to demonstrate the sequence of drawing". He suspects that there was often another mason, or mason's apprentice, standing nearby and watching as the drawing was taken through its various stages, beginning with a horizontal base line, then a centre line at right angles, and then some of the circles that are basic to the shape of what is being drawn. "Whoever drew the Weston Longville image knew this construction off by heart as part of their mental design portfolio."[52] A scenario of this kind may well explain some of the small inscribed drawings found on church walls.

49   Michael T. Davis, "On the drawing board", in Nancy Y. Wu (ed.), *Ad Quadratum: the Practical Application of Geometry in Medieval Architecture*, Aldershot: Ashgate, 2002, p. 190, quoting Roland Bechmann

50   Matthew Champion, "Medieval window sketch found at All Saints' Church, Weston Longville", *Norfolk Archaeology*, 46, 2012, pp. 383-6.

51   Matthew Champion, "Architectural inscriptions: discoveries in East Anglia", *Church Archaeology*, 16, 2012, pp. 65-8, especially, pp. 71-2

52   Laurie Smith, personal communication, 22 July 2013

CHAPTER 6

Locations of drawings

A little more needs to be said about the surfaces on which drawings were made and their locations within or near buildings, using documentary evidence as well as evidence from the sites of surviving drawing. The hard gypsum-ash (rather than lime-ash) plaster of the tracing floors at York and Wells is untypical. Stone floors and walls were probably more often used, usually coated with a thin lime plaster skim to provide a smoother surface for drawing. A plaster skim could also allow an earth or clay floor to be used for drawing.

Locations in which tracing floors are found indicate something of the conditions under which draughtsmen worked, and Table 1 summarises some relationships between location and drawing surface. The specialised construction of the floors at Wells and York, as well as their secluded locations in upper rooms, suggest the working environment of senior master masons with considerable status. Such were the leading craftsmen at York who are likely to have made drawings, notably the master masons William de Hoton in the fourteenth century and John Forman after 1500.

Some tracing houses are recorded in documents because the craftsmen working there were of the highest possible status – they were masons of the "King's works", sometimes dealing directly with the monarch himself. This applies to the masons recorded as working in the tracing houses at Knaresborough Castle,[53] and St Stephen's Chapel, Westminster.

The project at Knaresborough included building a keep or tower not only as a defensive structure but also as a luxuriously appointed residence (Figure 14). It was begun in 1307 on orders from Edward II, soon after his accession.

---

53   Peter Leach and Nikolaus Pevsner, *BOE, Yorkshire West Riding: Leeds, Bradford and the North*, London: Yale University Press, 2009, pp. 377-9.

Figure 14

*Knaresborough Castle, West Riding of Yorkshire: the King's Tower, built for
Edward II, 1307-12, with the master mason making use of a tracing house
nearby. The remains of ballflower ornament can be seen on the window
arch and jamb.*

(Photo: Pamela Maryfield)

Edward appointed Gilbert de Stapleton as clerk-of-works for the project, and Hugh de Tichemers
(or Titchmarsh) of London as master mason, with five other masons to assist. A lodge and tracing
house (*domus tracer*) were constructed for their use by the master carpenter William de Bocton.[54]
Nothing of this remains but the documentary evidence is clear, and the surviving stonework of
the tower shows details that would have had to be drawn out on a tracing floor, including a large
window with ballflower ornament that faced inwards, over the ward, and some intricate rib
vaulting inside.

---

54   R.A. Brown, H.M. Colvin and A.J. Taylor, *The History of the King's Works, vols. 1-2, The Middle Ages*,
       London: HMSO, 1963, vol. 1, p. 689.

A second documented tracing house (*trasura*) is recorded in the context of construction work at the Palace of Westminster in the fourteenth century. Oak boards imported from Baltic ports were sometimes bought for use as drawing boards, and were referred to as "Estrich boards" (East Reich boards). But when fifty Estrich boards were purchased in 1332 to make the Westminster tracing house larger, it sounds as if the tracing floor itself was made from such boards.[55] One other tracing floor was made at Ely Cathedral in 1387. It was next to a masons' lodge and had a surface paved in stone by men with typical occupational names: Peter Mason and John Leyer.[56] This should not be confused with the temporary tracing floor which some authors suggest was once in the Galilee Porch at Ely.[57]

The location of a tracing floor could sometimes depend on what it was being used for, because some drawings might be much larger than could be accommodated on a floor of limited size such as the one at York. That is why there has been speculation that the nave floor in Salisbury Cathedral may have been used for making drawings of the spire, and why it is likely that church floors were used in other places.

Church floors were also sometimes used simply because they were large, flat surfaces under cover. Places where this happened include Gisborough Priory, Yorkshire (as described in Chapter 3), and Vale Royal Abbey in Cheshire.

There are quite different questions to be asked about the small drawings or sketches to be seen on piers and walls in some churches. There are two kinds of location where they occur – sometimes they are in an easily accessible place to which anybody could have had access, and many in this kind of location are very rough and unlikely to be serious work by master masons. Examples in Cambridgeshire are in village churches at Barrington and Gamlingay, both on nave piers at about waist height.[58] These and a few other examples represent window tracery, but other drawings in similar locations represent heraldry, human figures, ships, and geometrical forms. Quite a number seem to have a ritual significance (as, for example, one drawing at Ashwell, Hertfordshire),[59] and some could have been made by people coming into the church to pray, or as pilgrims visiting shrines.[60] A few could be casual graffiti.

On the other hand, there are small drawings in places that could have only been reached while scaffolding was in place, or are in relatively inaccessible locations such as triforium galleries (as at Lincoln). Drawings in these places seem more likely to be the work of masons who were trying out design ideas in private, or teaching apprentices. As previously mentioned, blocks of dressed stone in builders' yards seem also to have been used for such purposes.

---

55   John Harvey, *Medieval Craftsmen*, London: Batsford, 1975, p.. 64.

56   Ibid, p. 77.

57   John Maddison, *Ely Cathedral: Design and Meaning*, Ely Cathedral Publications, 2000, pp. 56-7.

58   *MD*, p. 39.

59   *MD*, pp. 82-3

60   Maud Hurley, "Embodiment and devotion in English medieval church graffiti", Master of Studies dissertation, History Faculty, University of Oxford, 2013.

Another significant location for some drawings on walls (rather than floors) is when they were close to where construction was taken place, as was the case with drawings inside the west fronts of Byland Abbey (North Riding of Yorkshire) and Binham Priory (Norfolk). Such drawings may have been made so that they could be referred to by the builders.

Apart from locations such as these, the most significant medieval architectural drawings were made in tracing houses and on tracing floors, for which the evidence already discussed is summarised in Table 1.

Table 1

Tracing floors and tracing houses: a summary

Location of tracing floor	Surface used for drawing			
	Stone paving *(often with skim of lime plaster)*	*Plaster*	*Wooden boards*	*Other*
"Tracing house" separate from building site	Ely Cathedral (1387)[1,2]		St Stephen's Chapel, Palace of Westminster (1337)[2]	Knaresborough Castle; tracing floor of unknown type (1307)
Upper room in a church or monastery	Byland Abbey; above warming house, c.1200 (Chapter 3)	York Minster; above chapter house vestibule.[3]		Christchurch Priory; drawing on wall, not floor (Chapter 4)
	Canterbury Cathedral, corona? (Chapter 5)	Wells Cathedral; above north porch.[3]		
Floor of church	Gisborough Priory, nave (Chapter 3)			Vale Royal Abbey, Cheshire, transept; unknown floor surface.[5]
	Ely, possibly in Galilee Porch.[1]			
Other	Gloucester, now in Parliament Room (Chap. 2).			Kenilworth Abbey barn[6]

Notes

1. John Maddison, *Ely Cathedral: Design and Meaning*, Ely Cathedral Publications, 2000, p. 56.

2. John Harvey, *Medieval Craftsmen*, London: Batsford, 1975, pp. 64, 77.

3. *MD*, 2007, pp. 45-68.

5. John Maddison, "Master masons of the Diocese of Lichfield", *Transactions of the Lancashire and Cheshire Antiquarian Society*, 85, 1958.

6. Jennifer S. Alexander and H. Sunley. In L. Monckton and R.K. Morris, *Coventry: Medieval Art, Architecture and Archaeology*, BAACT, 33, 2011, pp. 327-343.

CHAPTER 7

Working drawings and geometry

Working drawings

One difficulty in writing about medieval architectural drawings is to decide which of many drawings found on the fabric of medieval buildings were really concerned with architectural design or construction. The large collection of drawings in the church at Ashwell, Hertfordshire, illustrates this especially clearly, because although there is at least one working drawing (of a lancet or slit window),[61] there are also sketches of buildings (including, supposedly, Old St Paul's in London) which have nothing to do with design or construction, and there are geometrical drawings that may have ritual significance.[62]

The most significant architectural drawings discussed here are probably the large design drawings and working drawings (*épures*) on tracing floors and walls which are mostly drawn to the actual size of what was to be constructed. Full-size drawing became less important once drawing to scale was widely practised, which was mainly a post-medieval development, but there were still situations where it was necessary to work designs out full-size in the traditional way, as can be illustrated by some drawings in post-medieval buildings (including some in the classical or Renaissance tradition).[63]

Among working drawings or *épures* that date from the thirteenth to early sixteenth centuries, the best collection in England is on the gypsum-plaster tracing floor at York Minster. One outline there is a fourteenth-century drawing for a large window that corresponds to windows actually constructed in the eastern arm of the Minster. Three other drawings are for the early sixteenth-century church of St Michael-le-Belfrey in York, which was a Minster responsibility. They include one of a flat, four-centred arch with profiles of mouldings on the arch and a quatrefoil pattern in its spandrel. The other two drawings for this church include an arched doorway and a window.[64] Also on the tracing floor are many fragments of other drawings which have not been identified, though some may be related to the west front of the Minster.

---

61   *MD*, p. 41 (Figure 2.6)

62   *MD*, pp. 40 and 82 (Figures 2.5 and 3.11)

63   *MD*, pp. 213-218.

64   *MD*, pp. 54, 130-3 (Figures 2.9, 5.6 and 5.7)

On the tracing floor at Wells Cathedral there is a drawing on a damaged part of the floor that shows a fragment of tracery in which there is an ogee shape under the arched head of a window. Detailed analysis, explained elsewhere,[65] has enabled the whole drawing to be reconstructed and to be identified with a window design used in the cathedral cloister around 1420 and later (Figure 15). Lines extending beyond the lowest part of the window drawing, not shown in this illustration, appear to represent the vaulted ceiling of the cloister walks. It is of particular interest that the draughtsman felt able to combine an elevation of window tracery with a plan view of the adjoining vault and an indication of vault curvature, all in one drawing.[66]

Other drawings on the tracing floor at Wells include long curves that may represent an arch or window opening, and what looks like a plan view of piers or responds, but these drawings have not been identified.

Among other examples of tracing-floor drawings mentioned in previous chapters were three or four at Gisborough Priory, North Riding of Yorkshire, the most detailed of which represents the plan view of a wall pier that was probably part of the west front of the church (Figure 9). Evidence has also been cited for a tracing floor at Byland Abbey, also in the North Riding. This was used in designing the large rose window for the abbey church.

On the four tracing floors discussed, therefore, three of them extant, there were several individual drawings, some of which can be identified with structures that were actually built and still stand.

Elsewhere, there are full-size design drawings on walls rather than floors, of which one of the most interesting, discussed in Chapter 4, is at Christchurch Priory. It is in an upper- floor room, and is a design for a window with "Geometrical" tracery such as was made for the ground floor in the same part of the building. It dates from the thirteenth century. Further east in Hampshire, there is a sixteenth-century drawing on a plastered wall in St Mary's, Old Basing which seems to be an accurate, if fragmentary, full-size drawing for the late Perpendicular window in the west wall of the nave.[67]

The location of a drawing within a building can be significant, as explained in the previous chapter, where mention was made of mural drawings inside the west walls of the monastic churches at Binham Priory, Norfolk,[68] and at Byland Abbey in the North Riding of Yorkshire (Chapter 3, above).

---

65   *MD*, pp. 65-73

66   This is explained with the aid of a series of drawings in *MD*, Figures 3.1-3.5, 9.3.

67   John Crook "New light on the history of St. Mary's Church, Old Basing, Hampshire: an incised design", *JBAA*, 154, 2001, pp. 92-132

68   Matthew Champion, "Tracery designs at Binham Priory", *English Heritage Historical Review*, 6, 2011, pp. 2-16.

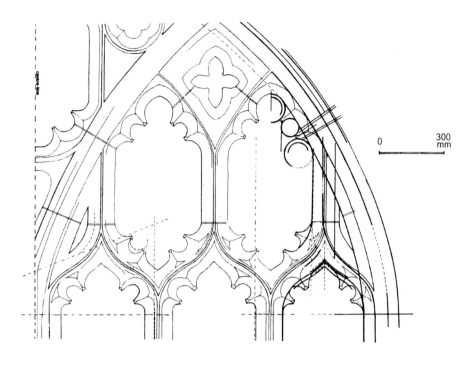

Figure 15

Wells Cathedral: reconstructed drawing of window detail on the tracing floor, and windows in the cloister

(Photo: Penny Jones, by kind permission of the Chapter of Wells Cathedral).

The drawing in Winchester Cathedral discussed in Chapter 4 is more problematic. It was not for a window and seems to be related to nearby blank quatrefoil decoration, but like the windows at Binham and Byland, the drawing is lower down on the same wall as the architectural detail to which it seems relevant (Figure 10), and could have been readily consulted by the builders. However, it differs in many ways from the completed work and more probably represents a rejected preliminary design.

Drawings on walls usually had different functions from those on tracing floors, and one in Salisbury Cathedral mentioned in Chapter 3 may be a presentation drawing made to show those who were commissioning the work what might be built. Hence this was not a working drawing. What remains is fragmentary, but can be reliably reconstructed from its 5-metre-long base line as representing a pair of two-light windows.[69]

These ten sites where accurate, full-size drawings have been found provide evidence of about fourteen individual drawings.[70] Of these, eight are on tracing floors and six on walls. Or perhaps, if unidentified fragments at Wells and York are counted, there is evidence at these places for more than twenty drawings. Most were probably made as part of a design process, except the presentation drawing at Salisbury, and it is very evident that different kinds of drawing had different functions. In this light, it is worth commenting that those cited from tracing floors at York and Wells were some distance from the relevant building site and up many stairs. They could not easily have been consulted by the craftsmen constructing the windows and other features to which they refer, nor are they likely to have been much used for making templates, because carrying the templates up and down the access stairs would have been difficult in both places.[71] Hence they most probably served mainly for working out details of designs.

Geometrical drawings

Apart from working drawings or design drawings set out to the precise size of the window or other feature that was being made, other medieval drawings discussed in previous chapters were mostly quite small, and some can be regarded as sketches or casual graffiti. Among the smaller drawing that may have had a purpose related to architectural design, several depict window tracery typical of the late thirteenth and early fourteenth centuries, and yet others, often the most significant, offer clues to the geometry used in design. This was nearly always what has been called "compass geometry".[72]

---

69   Rose Harris-Adamson, "Stonemasons' drawings on building fabric", *Archaeological Journal, 171*, 2014, pp. 258-88.

70   The ten sites are Ashwell (Herts.), Binham Priory (Norfolk), Byland and Gisborough (North Riding of Yorkshire), Christchurch, Old Basing and Winchester (Hants.), Salisbury, Wells and York.

71   Alexander Holton, "The working space of the medieval master mason: the tracing houses of York Minster and Wells Cathedral", *Proceedings of the Second International Construction History Congress*, London: Construction History Society, 2006, pp. 1579-97.

72   Laurie Smith, "Following the geometrical design path". In Peter Guillery (ed.), *Built from Below: British Architecture and the Vernacular*, London: Routledge, pp. 11-32; p. 12 on Ely.

In other words, the work of setting out a drawing depended on using compasses supplemented by a straight edge or ruler, and many of the constructions used depended on little more than the geometry of circles. In drawings of this kind, there were usually base lines and centre lines, but other details might all be formed by marking out arcs of circles. There are often prick marks to be seen where the metal compass points were placed. Drawings such as these, in which the geometrical process used in setting them out can be followed, include some at Ely,[73] a number in Lincoln Cathedral,[74] and one at Weston Longville in Norfolk.[75]

This is a subject that should be examined in detail as part of a fuller treatment of medieval drawing. But even in the absence of that extra detail, it is worth commenting that compass geometry was not only a practical technique, but could produce patterns expressing several kinds of meaning, some involving religious or cosmological symbolism. One of the more complex geometrical drawings at Ashwell (Hertfordshire) incorporates concentric circles combined with the monogram of Jesus, IHC or IHS, and clearly had ritual significance.[76] In other churches, small geometrical symbols are found to be concentrated in places traversed by people visiting shrines within the building.[77]

But the symbolism associated with circles was not restricted to drawings on walls and tracing floors. In the three Yorkshire monasteries discussed in Chapter 3, and in others too, there were enormous round windows whose meaning and significance has been much discussed.[78] At Byland Abbey, as indicated in Figure 7, part of a drawing for the rose window survives close to the site of the window. What can be added now is that, in one of the transept chapels at Byland there is a large circle pattern set out in the floor with plain mosaic tiles (Figure 16).

In several monasteries, especially again those of the Cistercian order, it seems that particular areas in the church, often including side chapels, were paved with tiles laid in a strictly geometrical manner. In several instances the tiles formed large roundels that echo, but do not copy, the patterns that would be seen in the large rose windows.

Byland is the only site at which a large part of the mosaic pavement survives, although much colour has been lost from the tiles due to weathering and wear of the glazed surface. But this survival, and evidence from other monastic ruins, raises questions about whether these large round patterns had some special meaning.[79] It also seems likely that the Byland tilers worked in several other places, and helped disseminate circular designs. Very similar floor patterns once existed at Meaux Abbey near the east coast, and at Sawley (or Salley) Abbey on the borders

73   *MD*, pp. 34 and 38 (Figures 2.1 and 2.3)

74   Jennifer S. Alexander, "Masons' marks and stone bonding". In Tim Tatton-Brown and Julian Munby (eds.), *The Archaeology of Cathedrals*, Oxford University Committee for Archaeology, 1996, pp. 219ff.

75   Matthew Champion, "Architectural inscriptions: discoveries in East Anglia", *Church Archaeology*, 16, 2012, pp. 65-80, especially pp. 71-3.

76   *MD*, p. 82, Figure 3.11.

77   Maud Hurley, *Embodiment and devotion in English medieval church graffiti*, Master of Studies dissertation, History Faculty, University of Oxford, 2013, p. 34, commenting on compass-drawn diagrams and cross shapes on the route leading to a shrine in Christchurch Cathedral, Oxford.

78   Painton Cowen, *The Rose Window: Splendour and Symbol*, London: Thames & Hudson, 2005

79   J. Stopford, *Medieval Floor Tiles of Northern England*, Oxford: Oxbow Books, 2005, pp. 18 and 107-8.

of Lancashire as well as at Newbattle Abbey near Dalkeith in Scotland. In all these places, the patterns formed by the tiles include abstract "compass geometry", notably in the ring of rosettes (or daisy wheels) on the floor at Byland (Figure 16).

Unfortunately there are no medieval drawings related to these remarkable and impressive floors to illustrate a connection between mosaic floor designs and rose windows. One can only say that, in other parts of the country too, there are twelfth- to fourteenth-century *floors* that display geometry of the kind used in *windows*, or in other parts of the same buildings. Notable examples are a transept floor and the floor of a chapel at Ely Cathedral.[80]

Even more impressive, at Canterbury Cathedral the "Opus Alexandrinum" floor in the Trinity Chapel displays intersecting square and circle patterns that are repeated in the south oculus window in the south-east transept.[81] Arguably the same patterns reflect the geometry behind the overall design of the Trinity Chapel.[82]

As to the remains of architectural drawings in the Yorkshire monasteries discussed here, it has to be said that they have nothing directly to do with the mosaic floor patterns in the same places except that a common heritage of compass geometry is expressed in all these things – drawings, rose windows and floor designs.

* * *

The main purpose of this book has been to establish how many and what kind of medieval architectural drawings survive in England, and to discuss how they were used – for it is clear that drawings had many different functions, which implies that there must have been vastly more of them than we can now find. It is understandable that most would be regarded as ephemeral, and not worth preserving once a building project was completed.

One thing learned from those drawings that do survive, however, is that very few were done freehand. Most were set out with compasses and a straight edge. That implies a system of practical geometry, rather different from the academic geometry inherited from the ancient Greeks. So with the knowledge of what medieval drawings survive to which this book may have contributed, the next subject on the agenda should probably be a detailed study of the geometry on which the drawings were based – a subject for which the last few paragraphs have suggested some pointers. With respect to drawings that survive on the continent, Robert Bork had shown how their geometry can be understood in an exemplary way.[83] In tackling the same subject in England, it will be desirable also to keep in mind the broader questions that have been raised here about rose windows, "geometrical" tracery, and mosaic floors.

---

80   Laurence Keen, "Tile pavements in Prior Crauden's chapel and the south transept". In Nicola Coldstream and Peter Draper, *Medieval Art and Architecture at Ely Cathedral*, BAACT, 2, 1979, pp. 47-57; also Laurie Smith, "Following the geometrical design path". In Peter Guillery (ed.), Built from Below, Abingdon: Routledge, 2011, pp. 11-32.

81   Jane Geddes, "The ferramenta of the oculi at Canterbury Cathedral". In Alixe Bovey (ed.), *Medieval Art, Architecture and Archaeology at Canterbury*, BAACT, 35, 2013, pp. 180-195 where p. 193 notes the geometric symbolism in the window and the floor and compares Cistercian rose windows in Yorkshire.

82   Jonathan Foyle, *Architecture of Canterbury Cathedral*, London, Scala Publishers, 2013, pp. 110-115.

83   Robert Bork, *The Geometry of Creation*, Farnham: Ashgate 2011.

Figure 16

Byland Abbey, North Riding of Yorkshire: Mosaic tile floor in a chapel opening off the south transept.

(photo: David Farrar)

GAZETTEER

A provisional list of places where architectural drawings have been recorded . It is likely that there are many other sites still to be identified.

Most entries refer to a medieval church in the place named. Also included are archives where drawings on parchment or paper are held. Dimensions of the smaller drawings are quoted as height by width.

Location	Surface: wall , floor, detached block, parchment	Size of drawing	Subject / function of drawing	References to where drawings have been published
BEDFORDSHIRE				
Leighton Linslade	wall	small, 13 x 7.6 cm	sketch, window tracery	Hine, 1930; Pevsner, 1968; this book, Figure 12
CAMBRIDGESHIRE				
Cambridge (Museum of Archaeology)	detached block of stone (clunch)	14.5 x 9.5 cm	window design showing geometry	Coulton 1928, p. 178; this book, Figure 12
Cambridge (Trinity College)	parchment	c. 50 x 30 cm, bound in Eadwine Psalter	record of monastic waterworks at Canterbury	Trinity College MS. r.17.1 f 284v/285. *MD*, Plate 23
Cambridge (Corpus Christi College)	paper (page of notebook)	freehand drawing c. 10 x 17 cm	profile of moulding on doorway	William Worcestre, Corpus MS., ed. Harvey, 1969. *MD*, Plate 11
Cambridge (Magdalene College)	parchment, bound into model book or sketchbook	page, 24 x 20 cm 4 drawings	2 drawings of moulding profiles; design for window tracery	MS. PL.1916, see M.R. James, 1925; *MD*, p. 127; this book Figure 2.

Location	Surface: wall, floor, detached block, parchment	Size of drawing	Subject / function of drawing	References to where drawings have been published
Ely Cathedral	wall	2 drawings: elevation, 80 x 48; window 55 x 40 cm	elevation of transept; two-light window; geometry	Pritchard, 1967, pp.37-42. *MD*, p. 38;
Barrington	pier	sketch, 20 x 8 cm	rough outline of window tracery	Coulton 1928, p. 179
Gamlingay	pier	sketch, 16 x 11 cm	rough freehand sketch	Coulton 1928, p. 179; *MD*, p. 39.
Whittlesford	wall	small rough sketch	Perp window	Coulton 1928, p. 179
GLOUCESTERSHIRE				
Gloucester Cathedral, Parliament Room	stone slab, formerly with plaster skim	several full size drawings of small mouldings	moulding profiles	Harris-Adamson, 2014; pp. 265-7; this book, Figures 1, 3-5, cover
Gloucester Cathedral, tower	external stone wall	full size	setting-out lines for window	Harris-Adamson, 2014, p. 270
Gloucester Cathedral, Lady Chapel	back of niche in reredos	full size, 60 x 29 cm	outline of sculpture intended for niche	*MD*, p. 123
Acton Court (house), Iron Acton	plastered wall	full size, 200 x 200 cm	oriel window, with other subjects.	Rodwell & Bell, 2004, pp. 271-5; *MD*, p. 136
HAMPSHIRE				
Christchurch Priory	plastered wall	full size (200 x 200 cm)	design of window for chantry chapel	Crook, 2001, p. 129; Figure 11 in this book
Old Basing	plastered wall	full size	west window of church	Crook, 2001, pp. 92-132
Winchester Cathedral	stone wall	60 x 60 cm	design for blank quatrefoils	Figure 10 in this book; Hurley, 2013.
Winchester, St Cross, north aisle of nave	wall	geometrical drawing, 70 x 70 cm	geometry	Harris-Adamson, 2014, p. 271
HERTFORDSHIRE				
Ashwell, south aisle, W end, wall facing south	stone (clunch) wall	window drawing, 40 x 30 cm	elevation of window with plan of opening and splays	*MD*, p.41

Location	Surface: wall, floor, detached block, parchment	Size of drawing	Subject / function of drawing	References to where drawings have been published
Ashwell, inside base of tower	stone (clunch) wall	pictorial sketch of church with spire (St Paul's?); 30 x 40 cm; other drawings nearby	record of existing building	Hine, 1951, p. 208 *MD*, p. 40
Ashwell, nave	several piers	example, 40 x 50 cm	circles with IHS monogram; rough sketches of towers	*MD*, p. 82
Offley	wall, window splay	small sketch	rough, incomplete outline of window tracery	Coulton 1928, p. 179
KENT				
Canterbury Cathedral, Corona	drawings on stair	c. 40 x 40 cm	sketch of tracery	Huitson, 2014, p. 135
Dartford (Holy Trinity)	drawings on detached block, later used in wall	17 x 17 cm, upside-down	window tracery	Bailey, 1997, pp. 46-7; this book Figure 13
LINCOLNSHIRE				
Lincoln Cathedral, Angel Choir triforium	stonework	four small drawings	geometry related to Bishop's window	Alexander, 1996; Harris-Adamson, 2014, p. 269
Lincoln Cathedral, Longland Chapel	originally on detached blocks?	vesica, 22 x 14; geometry of trefoil 24 x 20 cm	geometry, related to tracery	Alexander, 1996
LONDON				
British Library, MS. Cotton, Augustus, II, 1	vellum	drawing probably by William Vertue, 58 x 39 cm	design for tomb, partly in perspective	Marks and Williamson, 2003, catalogue nos. 27 and 109.
Victoria and Albert Museum, RIBA drawings; Smithson Collection, IV/1	paper (with watermark)	elevation 96 x 29 cm	design for Bishop Fox's chantry, c.1515	*MD*, p. 169; for this and other late medieval drawings, see Girouard, 1962, pp. 167-9
Southwark Cathedral	stone	full-size	drawing for positioning stone	Willis, 1842, quoted by Branner, 1997, p. 67

Location	Surface: wall, floor, detached block, parchment	Size of drawing	Subject / function of drawing	References to where drawings have been published
NORFOLK				
Binham Priory	stone walls, piers, respond	half size and full size	west window, drawings for design and reference	Champion, 2011; Champion 2012b, pp. 68-70
Castle Acre Priory	plaster, wall	now destroyed	window tracery	Coulton, 1928; no visual record
Caston	timber, rear of rood screen	60 x 60 cm, possibly full size	design of tracery for rood screen	Champion, 2012b, p. 76
East Harling	timber, rear of screen	100 x 150 cm	fragment, arch shape	Champion, 2012b, p. 77
Gateley	timber, bench end	55 x 35 cm	curvilinear tracery fragment	Champion, 2012b, p. 78
Marsham	timber, rear of rood screen	60 x 40 cm over-lapping 2 boards	fragment, arch shape	Champion, 2012b, p. 75
Ringland	timber, rear of rood screen	14 x 18 cm	circles, geometrical tracery design	Champion, 2012b, p. 75
Scole	stone	two sketches, each 15 x 20 cm	rough outlines of intersecting tracery	Champion, 2012b, p. 73
Weston Longville	stone, south arcade	2 drawings, 15 x 15 cm	geometry for curvilinear tracery	Champion, 2012a; Champion, 2012b, pp. 71-2
SOMERSET				
Wells Cathedral	plaster tracing floor	full size	window tracery, plan view of vault, pier and respond	this book, Figure 15; *MD*, pp. 65-70, 222
SUFFOLK				
Blythburgh	timber surface; parclose screen	50 x 50 cm, full size?	design for coving below rood loft	Champion, 2012b, p. 77
Polstead	plaster/stone piers and wall	35 cm x 100 cm (circles 35 cm dia.)	geometrical setting-out for painting	*MD*, Plate 24
WARWICKSHIRE				
Kenilworth Abbey barn	tracing floor	no details of drawings		J. S. Alexander and H. Sunley, 2011
WILTSHIRE				
Salisbury Cathedral	stone wall	large square with inscribed octagon, 122 x 122 cm	geometry	Harris-Adamson, 2014, p. 272

Location	Surface: wall , floor, detached block, parchment	Size of drawing	Subject / function of drawing	References to where drawings have been published
Salisbury Cathedral, south aisle of nave	stone wall	full-size, on 500 cm base line	presentation drawing: windows in north porch	Harris-Adamson, 2014, pp. 281-5
WORCESTERSHIRE				
Worcester (Record Office)	parchment	38 x 106 cm	elevation, timber-framed house	Charles & Down, 1970-2; *MD*, Plate 29
YORKSHIRE NORTH RIDING and CITY OF YORK				
York Minster	gypsum plaster tracing floor	4 or 5 idenitfiable drawings, full size	tracery, doorway spandrels, arch	Harvey, 1968, pp. 1-8; *MD*, pp. 53-7, 131-2
Byland Abbey	former tracing floor; drawing on west wall	full size; of rose window	design, template making, reference during construction	Harrison and Barker, 1987; this book Figure 7
Gisborough Priory	floor, stone paved	full size	design: piers, shafts, mouldings	D.H. Heslop, 1995
Jervaulx Abbey	stone surface on base or respond	full size	drawing to guide positioning stone	Fergusson, 1979; this book Figure 8.
YORKSHIRE WEST RIDING				
Ripon Cathedral	flat stone surface on top of pier	full-size	drawing for positioning stone	Forster, Robson, & Deadman, 1993, p.89

Sources referred to in Gazetteer

Alexander, J. S., 1996, "Masons' marks and stone bonding". In: Tim Tatton-Brown and J. Munby (eds.), *The Archaeology of Cathedrals*, Oxford University Committee for Archaeology, pp. 219-236.

Alexander, J. S., and Sunley, H., 2011, "Kenilworth Abbey Barn". In: L. Monckton and R.K. Morris, *Coventry: Medieval Art, Architecture and Archaeology*, BAACT, 33, 2011, pp. 327-343.

Bailey, John, 1997, *Church Archaeology*, vol. 1, pp. 46-7.

Branner, Robert, 1997, "Origin of Gothic architectural drawing". In: Lynn T. Courtenay (ed.), *The Engineering of Medieval Cathedrals*, Aldershot: Ashgate, 1997, pp. 63-80.

Champion, M., 2011, "Tracery design at Binham Priory", *English Heritage Historical Review*, 6, pp. 2-15.

Champion, M, 2012a, "Medieval window sketch at All Saints Church, Weston Longville," *Norfolk Archaeology*, 46, 2012a, pp. 383-6.

Champion, M., 2012b, "Architectural inscriptions: discoveries in East Anglia", *Church Archaeology*, 16, pp. 65-80.

Charles, F.W.B., and Down, K., 1970-72, *Transactions of Worcestershire Archaeological Society*, 3rd series, 3, 1970-72, pp. 67-79.

Coulton, G.G., 1928, *Art and the Reformation*, Oxford, Blackwell.

Crook, J, 2001, "New light on the history of St. Mary's Church, Old Basing, Hampshire: an incised design", *JBAA*, 154, 2001, pp. 92-132.

Fergusson, Peter, 1979, "Notes on two Cistercian engraved designs", *Speculum*, 54, 1979, pp. 1-17.

Forster, B., Robson, B., and Deadman. J., 1993, *Ripon Cathedral: its History and Architecture*, York: William Sessions.

Girouard, Mark, 1962, "The Smythson collection of the RIBA", *Architectural History*, 5, pp. 167-9.

Harris-Adamson, Rose, 2014, "Stone masons' drawings on building fabric", *Archaeological Journal*, 171, pp. 258-88.

Harrison, S., and Barker, P., 1987, "Byland Abbey...the west front and rose window reconstructed", *JBAA*, 140, 1987, pp. 134-151.

Harvey, J.H., 1968, "The tracing floor of York Minster", reprinted in Lynn T. Courtenay (ed.), *The Engineering of Medieval Cathedrals*, Aldershot: Ashgate, 1997, pp. 81-6.

Harvey, J.H. (ed.), 1969, *Itineraries of William Worcestre*, Oxford: Clarendon Press.

Heslop, D.H., 1995, "Excavations within the church of the Augustinian priory at Gisborough, Cleveland", *YAJ*, 67, pp. 51-74.)

Hine, Reginald, 1930. MSS. held by the Society of Antiquaries, London.

Hine, Reginald, 1951, *Relics of an Un-Common Attorney*, London: Dent.

Huitson, Toby, 2014, *Stairway to Heaven*, Oxford: Oxbow.

Hurley, Maud, 2013, "Embodiment and devotion in English medieval church graffiti", Master of Studies dissertation, History Faculty, University of Oxford.

James, M.R., 1925, "An English medieval sketchbook", *Walpole Society*, 13, pp. 1-17.

Marks, Richard, and Williamson, Paul (eds.), 2003, *Gothic: Art for England*, V&A Museum, 2003.

Pevsner, Nikolaus, 1968, *BOE Bedfordshire, Huntingdon, and Peterborough*, Penguin.

Pritchard, Violet, 1967, *English Medieval Graffiti*, Cambridge University Press.

Rodwell, K., and Bell, R., 2004, *Acton Court: the Evolution of an early Tudor Courtier's House*, London: English Heritage.

Willis, Robert, 1842, "On construction of the vaults of the Middle Ages", Transactions of the *RIBA*, I, pt. 2, pp. 1-69, quoted by Branner, 1997, see above.

Worcestre, William, *Itineraries*, MS. held by Corpus Christi College, Cambridge, ed. John Harvey, Oxford: Clarendon Press, 1969